CRAZY CHOICES

CHOICES

FOR

9 YEAR OLDS

A serious talk about (under)pants

Crazy Choices are designed to bamboozle – but some children may be more bamboozled than others. Bathing suit or swimming costume? Washroom or toilet? There's more: sandwiched between the Greek mythology and particle physics you'll also find the occasional poo(p), strategic ~~bogey~~ booger and even a mission-critical ~~bum~~ butt or two. I've mixed and matched to keep everyone happy, I hope – but some choices, words and spelling may lead to a little extra head-scratching!

There's only one thing for it: embrace the bum! Savo~~u~~r the hum~~ou~~r, and don't tell yo~~ur~~ ~~head teacher~~ (or m~~u~~m). oops principal

Design: Fanni Williams / thehappycolourstudio.com
www.matwaugh.co.uk

Produced by Big Red Button Books,
a division of Say So Media Ltd.

ISBN: 978-1-915154-24-8

Published: November 2022
Updated: March 2023

CRAZY CHOICES

MAT WAUGH
ILLUSTRATIONS BY DAVE HALL

How to play
Crazy Choices

A book you can PLAY?
What will they think of next?

 One-player mode

Take book. Read book. Laugh, read bits to your
grandpa or cat and say, "Eurgh, that's disgusting!"
Test yourself with the Tricky Trivia questions.
Finish book. Send winning lottery ticket to me,
the author (optional, highly recommended).

 Two-player mode

Grab a friend and a pen and dive into Brainy's Tricky
Trivia starting on page 8. For each question, discuss and
make your choice: the same or different, you decide!

Each option has a score, depending on whether it's a
brainwave or a truly terrible plan. Turn the page to
find out who chose the winner and who picked the
stinker. Now add your points to the scorecard on
page 133. Who's Yoda, and who's useless?

You're all set. Now go crazy!

Mat

MAKE A CRAZY CHOICE!

Blow up balloons with a puff adder...

...squeeze oranges with a boa constrictor?

MAKE A CRAZY CHOICE!

Arm wrestle a gorilla...

OR

...play board games with a cheetah?

CRAZY CHOICES FOR **9** YEAR OLDS

MAKE A CRAZY CHOICE!

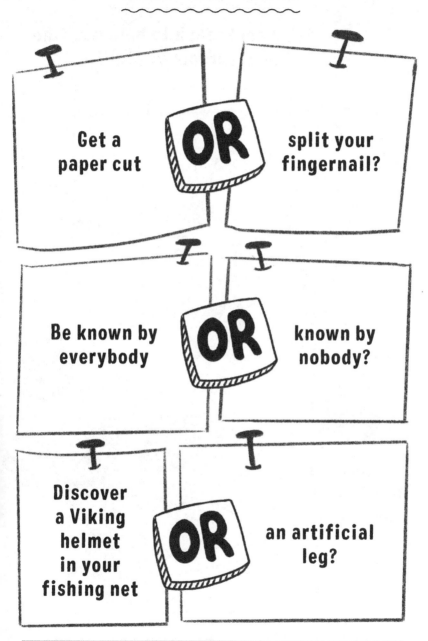

Get a paper cut **OR** split your fingernail?

Be known by everybody **OR** known by nobody?

Discover a Viking helmet in your fishing net **OR** an artificial leg?

BRAINY'S TRICKY TRIVIA!

Ask a cockroach to help you find the bathroom at night...

see page 10

OR

...use the light of your forehead?

BRAINY'S TRICKY TRIVIA!

Go to sleep at the end of an airport runway **OR** next to the monkey enclosure at the zoo?

P11

Count the trees on Earth **OR** the stars in the galaxy?

P12

Be led into battle by General Sherman **OR** Major Oak?

P13

COCKROACH vs FOREHEAD

CONFUSED? Me too. This take a bit of explaining. Let's start with the cockroach: this little critter can detect light 100 times better than you. So when it's pitch black for you, a cockroach is saying, **"WHAT'S THE PROBLEM?"** They'll never bump into the toilet, that's for sure.

But you have your own secret trick. In 2009, scientists discovered that humans glow, particularly from the head and shoulders. Result! Sadly, the light we give off is 1,000 times fainter than humans can see. This makes your bonce totally useless as a torch.

An artist's impression of you in the bathroom at night

Cockroach `3pts` **Forehead** `0pts`

The answer? Grab a cockroach's tiny leg and ask him to take you for a pee.

RUNWAY vs ZOO

They're both noisy places, but which is worse? Noise is measured in decibels (dB): higher decibels mean a louder sound. A jet engine is about 150dB if you get close enough. Don't do this — you'll **BURST YOUR EARDRUMS**. Ouch.

Here's another silly thing to do: annoy a troop of black howler monkeys from South America. Around sunset they start to howl at **140dB.** The loudest human yell is about 120dB. (To find out what that sounds like, jump in a cold shower).

But before you snuggle up at the zoo, here's one more thing. As far as we know, jet engines have never thrown poo at anyone. Howler monkeys, however...

Runway (-1 pt) **Zoo** (-3 pts)
Both are silly – but only one choice is smelly.

TREES vs STARS

Go somewhere really dark and peer into the night sky. How many stars can you see? Millions, right? Errm, no. Only around 9,000 stars can be seen without a telescope. And our big fat Earth gets in the way, so you can only see 4,500 of these at once. But out there in our galaxy — the Milky Way — you'll find **100 BILLION** more. If you're a fan of zeros, that's 100,000,000,000.

Too easy? Count leafy things. There are around **THREE TRILLION** trees: 3,000,000,000,000. But we need to look after those trees and we're not

doing a very good job: humans chop down around 15 billion of them every year, and only 5 billion grow back.

Trees `1pts` **Stars** `3pts`

Count stars, then rush back to look after the trees!

GENERAL vs MAJOR

These army leaders can often be found **ROOTED** to the spot, **BARKING** instructions. Why? Because they're two of our three trillion trees*. **GENERAL SHERMAN** is the world's biggest, and you'll find him — sorry, it — in California's Sequoia National Park. This 83m whopper is named after the real General Sherman who fought in the American Civil War. It's around 2,500 years old, although nobody can be sure.

The Major Oak is also named after an army fellow. It's just 1,000 years old. But it's England's most famous tree, because legend tells that **ROBIN HOOD** and **HIS MERRY MEN** sheltered beneath Major Oak's huge canopy.

* Yes, this is an awful joke. No, I won't apologise.

General 4 pts Major 7 pts

General is bigger, but the Major could tell better stories!

MAKE A CRAZY CHOICE!

Be afraid of pencils  be afraid of words that rhyme?

Live in the future  live in the past

You choose the date. The Stone Age? 3000AD? Next week?

Try landing a plane without any lessons  skydive?

MAKE A CRAZY CHOICE!

Be abducted by aliens...

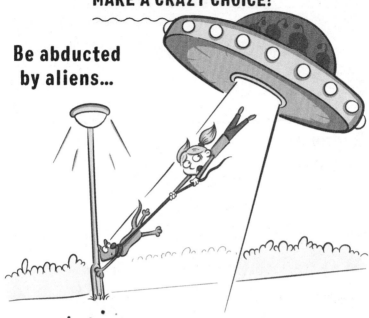

OR

...discover that your parents are alien?

Dodge a meteorite shower...

OR

...stand in a sandstorm in your underpants?

MAKE A CRAZY CHOICE!

Clean a toilet to earn your favourite meal **OR** never eat your favourite meals again?

Have your own family anthem, to be sung every day at dawn **OR** have your own family flag, to fly from the roof of your car?

Eat only food that begins with the first letter of your first name **OR** the first letter of your surname?

MAKE A CRAZY CHOICE!

Find out the biggest CIA secrets **OR** find out how any magic trick works?

Have a giant treehouse in your garden **OR** a tree growing through your bedroom?

Get pinched every time you say a word beginning with 'q' **OR** every time you say 'umm'

MAKE A CRAZY CHOICE!

Skip everywhere for a week...

OR

...walk backwards?

MAKE A CRAZY CHOICE!

Fall into an ant nest...

OR

...into a patch of nettles?

MAKE A CRAZY CHOICE!

Roll a six-sided die to decide how many days you'll go to school next week

OR

to decide how many presents you'll get on your birthday?

Skip meals without getting hungry

OR

not get thirsty?

Have eyes in the back of your head (like your teacher!)

OR

a nose at the end of your finger?

MAKE A CRAZY CHOICE!

Salute the next teacher you meet  **blow raspberries at your mum?**

Be a fly on the wall in the White House  **Buckingham Palace?**

> A fly on the wall watches everything that goes on without being seen!

Spend a day in a stormtrooper's helmet **or talk like Darth Vader for a week?**

MAKE A CRAZY CHOICE!

Dream about monsters...

...dinosaurs?

BRAINY'S TRICKY TRIVIA!

Share a bedroom with a dolphin...

OR

...a snail?

see page 26

Spend a night in a shed, listening to rhubarb **OR** a night on a submarine, listening to the mysterious Bloop? P28

Write a poem about a silver wolf with wounds that you glimpsed **OR** about a dangerous, angry angel? P27

Go on a school trip to The Museum of Smelly Socks **OR** the Museum of Underpants? P30

DOLPHIN vs SNAIL

Most gardeners think that **snails** sleep all day and munch their lettuces all night. You'd never get to sleep with all that chewing. But snails don't really do our 'night and day' thing. Sometimes they'll be awake for **15 HOURS**. But if they get stressed, they go to sleep for up to **three years.** Imagine how much school they miss.

A dolphin would be good fun, but you wouldn't get much rest. They send one half of their brain to sleep at a time, while the other half keeps an eye out for danger. And then they'll start clicking, groaning, whistling and yelping with their dolphin chums and **CAN YOU JUST KEEP THE NOISE DOWN PLEASE, DOLLY!**

Dolphin (-2 pts) **Snail** 2 pts

Snails don't say much – and you'll definitely beat them to the bathroom!

WOLF vs ANGEL

The **CRAZY CHOICES POETRY COMPETITION** is open! All you have to do is write one of these poems and send it to me using my email, which you'll find in the back of this book. oh, and it has to rhyme.

Now you're in trouble. Because lots of words don't have a rhyme including **ANGEL, PURPLE, WOLF, WOUNDS, GLIMPSE, SILVER** or — hang on, there's a farmer on the phone. She always calls when I'm busy.

"YOU'VE LOST YOUR chilvers? THAT'S SAD. HOW DO YOU PRONOUNCE CHILVER? YOU'RE SURE? OH DEAR."

Right, so, ahem. There's a problem. Silver rhymes with chilver — that's a female lamb. Still, the **OTHER** words don't rhyme with anything. Probably.

Wolf `5pts` Angel `5pts`
Get a thousand bonus points if you write the poem!

RHUBARB vs SUBMARINE

Using my incredible mind-reading skills I predict that you're not a big fan of rhubarb, the vegetable that looks like purple celery.

To be fair, not many nine year olds are keen on it. Perhaps it's because the pudding made by your grandmother tastes as if it's dissolving your teeth — oh, hello, grandma! No, I didn't mean YOU!

But you'd be even less keen on it if you spent a night in the Rhubarb Triangle, a small, mysterious area in the North of England. This is where you'll find the forcing sheds and shadowy people harvesting rhubarb by CANDLELIGHT. And listen to the prisoners, oops, I mean the rhubarb: it's growing so fast that you can hear it squeak and pop.

Bad Things happen in here (to the rhubarb)

So let's escape to the southern Pacific where scientists first heard a strange underwater noise, which they nicknamed **The Bloop.** This loud and

unusual noise could be heard in places that were thousands of miles apart. Was it someone testing underwater weapons? Or a giant shark species nobody had ever seen?

The brightest marine experts took **EIGHT YEARS** to work out that The Bloop was just the sound of icebergs cracking and breaking away in Antarctica. Phew.

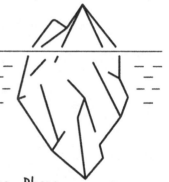

Rhubarb `5pts` **The Bloop** `2pts`

*Those sheds sound terrifying
(but at least you get pudding for breakfast).*

SOCKS vs UNDERPANTS

Only one of these is a real museum, but did you make the right crazy choice?

We've searched the globe and nobody has been crazy enough to open a **MUSEUM OF SMELLY SOCKS**. Although sometimes my children could open one in their bedrooms (poooooo!).

But there IS a museum of (under)pants. And it's not just any underwear — it's celebrity undies. Why would you want to look at those? I have absolutely no idea. But if you do, then rush to the museum in Hollywood. Take spare underwear, in case you get famous on the way and need to donate it.

Could the person who has left their pants on my page please remove them. Thanks

Socks (-4 pts) Underpants (-4 pts)

There are no winners with these two terrible ideas.

MAKE A CRAZY CHOICE!

Fly like a bird...

...swim like a seal?

Wake up and think that it's Christmas every day (except when it is) **OR** wake up every day thinking that you have a test (except on test days)?

Live without TV **OR** live without video games?

Be great at winning arguments **OR** fantastic at making peace?

MAKE A CRAZY CHOICE!

Have the eyesight of an eagle...

...be able to turn your head right round, like an owl?

MAKE A CRAZY CHOICE!

Get nipped by a crab...

OR

...stung by a wasp?

MAKE A CRAZY CHOICE!

Turn anything to gold with a touch, like King Midas make things disappear by looking at them?

Live in a glass box a hot air balloon?

Own a huge hot tub with disco lights  a private observatory?

If you've already got one of these, can I come round please?

MAKE A CRAZY CHOICE!

Wrestle a rhino  **grapple with a gorilla?**

Eat all your meals from a bucket  **have them thrown at you by catapult?**

Lose a lobster in the library  **a bison in the bakery?**

MAKE A CRAZY CHOICE!

Get pins and needles in your leg...

OR

...an itchy ear?

BRAINY'S TRICKY TRIVIA!

See the world speeded up **OR** in slow motion?

p41

Paint your bedroom Mummy Brown **OR** Emerald Green?

p42

Get your invisible ink from the kitchen **OR** the bathroom?

p43

DONKEY vs RAT

Two **delicious** choices. How will you choose?

Donkey milk has been popular for thousands of years. Cleopatra bathed in it, but only when it had gone sour (yuck). She believed it made her skin 𝕊𝕞𝕠𝕠𝕥𝕙𝕖𝕣 and even today, donkey milk is used in some face creams. Babies without mothers were even taken to the donkey to suckle (drink the milk). So a donkey milkshake would be a healthy choice!

But what about rats? A few years ago, a celebrity suggested that we could use them for milk. They **ARE** mammals, but they only produce a teaspoon a day. It would take you a month to collect a cupful. Nobody has ever tried — but perhaps it's worth the wait?

Donkey 3pts **Rat** 0pts

If you don't drink it, rub it on your face instead!

SPEED UP vs SLOW DOWN

Think how fast those boring lessons would go if you could set the world to **2x** or even **3x** normal speed! But then your birthday party would be over in a flash as well...

Perhaps you'd be better choosing to see things in Slow... motion. Birds, dogs and other small creatures see the world this way. Even when you're dashing around, to them you're a lumbering beast. That's why they find it so easy to run rings round you or steal your fries and fly away (pesky seagulls, I'm looking at you!)

Speed up `2pts` **Slow down** `8pts`

Max points for taking it slow. I bet you chose fast!

BROWN vs GREEN

These lovely-sounding colours are definitely not lovely! **MUMMY BROWN,** for instance, is not the colour of the chocolate that mummy likes to eat. (Actually, maybe it is, but that's a coincidence.) If I told you that its other name is Egyptian Brown, would that help?

This colour was very popular with artists around 200 years ago and was made from **MINCED-UP EGYPTIAN MUMMIES.** Human or cat, it didn't matter — whatever could be found. Artists stopped using it for two reasons: they found out how it was made and said, **"Yuck!"** And the world ran out of mummies that people could turn into paint.

So perhaps Emerald Green might be cheerier? It was also called **PARIS GREEN.**

It was used by some of the world's most famous artists including Turner, Monet and Van Gogh. Your clue might be that a tin of this jolly green paint also had another word on it: **POISON**. It was used to kill rats in Paris, and that's how it got its name.

Brown (-4 pts) **Green** (-4 pts)

Isn't red a lovely colour? Or orange? Or anything else?!

KITCHEN vs BATHROOM

If you have a secret to send, both of these are actually a good place to get started (as long as you can find the ink!). Let's explain.

One common way to write a message in invisible ink is to use an **ACID**. Dip a cocktail stick or something pointy in the acid and write your message. The acid dries to become invisible, but it will also make ➡

➡ the paper weak. When your letter arrives, the other spy — you **are** a spy, aren't you? — will heat the letter (a radiator will do). The first bits to go brown, or burn, will be

Warning: this is what happens if you wash your face with invisible ink.

the thin parts of the paper. Your message will magically appear. Amazing!

Heh? What's that? **WHERE DO YOU GET A POT OF ACID?** Ah! that's easy: look in the kitchen. You could use onion juice, lemon juice or even milk.

In the bathroom, there's an acid that prisoners have used to write secret letters. It's always available, with fresh supplies every few hours. Can you guess?

Yes, it's your own PEE!

I love shouting that out loud to annoy grown-ups. But I suggest you experiment with milk — otherwise I'll be in BIG trouble with your parents!

EXTRA SPY TIP: has your teacher ever asked you to *read between the lines* of a story? They want you to find a hidden meaning in the words. But this used to mean something very different. Prisoners used to write boring letters in pencil or pen, because they knew that the guards would read them. And then they'd write the secret bits — in wee, or milk — between the lines.

DEAR MUM, THE FOOD HERE IS LOVELY AND THE
Mum! Land the helicopter in the prison yard
GUARDS ARE VERY NICE.
at 9pm tonight. Bring snacks, I'm starving!

Kitchen 5pts **Bathroom** 1pt
Nobody wants to get whiffy secret letters!

MAKE A CRAZY CHOICE!

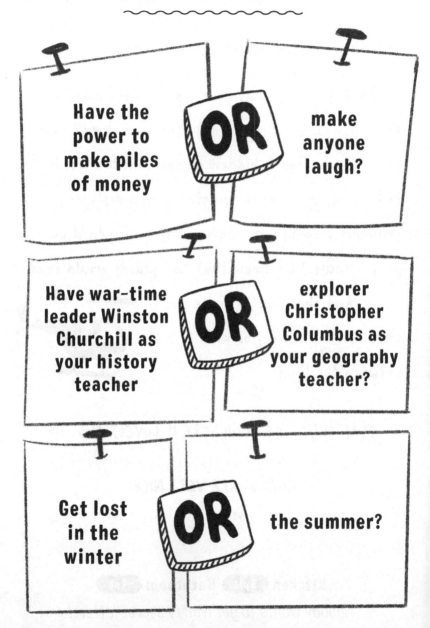

Have the power to make piles of money **OR** make anyone laugh?

Have war-time leader Winston Churchill as your history teacher **OR** explorer Christopher Columbus as your geography teacher?

Get lost in the winter **OR** the summer?

MAKE A CRAZY CHOICE!

Fight with a raptor...

OR

...a pterodactyl?

MAKE A CRAZY CHOICE!

Fight with twenty-six sharks the size of goldfish...

OR

...one goldfish the size of twenty-six sharks?

MAKE A CRAZY CHOICE!

Make any dream you have on Mondays come true **OR** dream about chocolate every night?

Stop all wars **OR** halt global warming?

Accidentally call your teacher mummy (or mommy, or daddy!) **OR** hold your parent's hand at your birthday party?

Spend a month eating all your meals with a blindfold on  eating your meals with your plate behind you

Win 10 extra presents by spelling Caribbean and Czechoslovakia (no peeking!)  by holding your arms out like a zombie for 3 minutes?

Fail and you lose ALL your presents!

Shout 'Fire!' whenever you see something red  yell "I love custard!" whenever you see something yellow?

MAKE A CRAZY CHOICE!

Cross the Sahara on a camel...

...cross Antarctica on a penguin?

Go to war before school **OR** play basketball? → p54

Have holes in your eyelids **OR** a tail? → p60

Live as long as a skyscraper **OR** a parrot? → p56

BRAINY'S TRICKY TRIVIA!

Leave your baby brother with a wolf...

OR

...a sumo wrestler?

see page 58

WAR vs BASKETBALL

If you want to be on time, choose a war — you could be finished in **40 MINUTES**. But pick basketball and you might find yourself in The Late Book (each game lasts 48 minutes).

So how do you fight a war in the time it takes my children to do their teeth? For that, we need to open up the dusty history books to learn about the Anglo-Zanzibar war, fought in 1896.

Zanzibar is a gorgeous island of sandy beaches and palm trees, just off the east coast of Africa.

Back then, Zanzibar was a protectorate of Britain — it was protected (and controlled) by Britain. But it still had a **SULTAN,** or ruler. And when the old ruler died, a new Sultan named Khalid took his place in the palace. But the

British didn't like Khalid, and demanded that he give up his place for someone else. Khalid refused, and prepared to defend the palace. The British set a deadline to surrender, or they would attack. **TICK TOCK, TICK TOCK...** the deadline came and went.

Forty minutes later, 500 of Khalid's defenders had been killed. Just one British sailor was injured. Khalid and his forces were thrown out, and the British installed a *puppet government* (this means a government that will do anything you want them to do, like puppets).

When someone is secretly in control, we say they're 'pulling the strings'

War (-3 pts) **Basketball** (3 pts)
Play basketball: nobody gets hurt and it's more fun!

SKYSCRAPER vs PARROT

Cities around the world are filled with SKYSCRAPERS. Land is expensive, so it's cheaper to build **UP!**

There are lots of huge structures that have been

around for hundreds or even thousands of years: castles, cathedrals and even the

PYRAMIDS. So will that

apartment block down the road still be there in a thousand years?

Probably not. We've only been building skyscrapers for about 100 years. And although they're built to last, we're already taking some of them down — on average, after just

42 years.

And as these towers get dismantled, listen carefully

Before you were born, most buildings were knocked down with 'wrecking balls' like this. Fun, but very, very messy!

and you might hear the sound of laughter. That's the parrots. They saw the skyscrapers being built, and they'll be around long after they've gone. Some live longer than your average grandpa.

Now listen again, really carefully. Do you hear that? It's the sound of an Australian **TORTOISE** called

Harriet in 2006: artist's impression
(Artist is 6 years old)

Harriet. She's 175 years old*, and she's laughing** at the parrot and his shrinky-dinky lifespan. A different tortoise is believed to have lived for **255 years.**

* I've done some research. Harriet died in 2006, so it must have been another tortoise. Although the bit about her being 175 years old is true.

** I've done some more research. It turns out that tortoises can't laugh. I must have been imagining it.

Skyscraper `1pt` **Parrot** `4 pts`

Parrots are four times better than skyscrapers. FACT.

WOLF vs SUMO

Do you know the story of The Jungle Book? The man-cub Mowgli is adopted by a pack of wolves, led by the wise and noble Akela. But **COULD THIS HAPPEN IN REAL LIFE** — would wolves make good parents (or babysitters)?

No.

That was easy, wasn't it? Wolves are pretty scared of humans, but you still wouldn't want to get too close to one. Also, they howl a LOT.

What about a sumo wrestler?

Sumo is the national sport of Japan, where professional wrestlers put on huge amounts of weight to be able to win this battle of strength and wits. Here's where it gets a bit weird. Every year, parents take their **BABIES** to shrines across Japan

and hand them over to a wrestler... to make them CRY (the babies, not the wrestlers).

A sumo wrestler's belt is 10m long!

Sometimes there's even a race to see *which baby will cry first,* or loudest. Wrestlers stamp about, shout and jiggle the babies around. They don't do anything cruel — just enough to get the babies wailing.

Why would anyone do that? Because the parents hope that God will hear the cries, and the baby will then grow up big and strong.

And those sumo wrestlers? They're just **BIG SOFTIES** when they're not competing — the perfect babysitters!

Wolf (-2 pts) **Sumo** `3 pts`

Don't trust a wolf. Just ask the three little pigs!

HOLES vs TAIL

You don't have to decide... **YOU ALREADY HAVE BOTH!**

That's not quite right: you **had** a tail, but you lost it. Because when you were just a tiny embryo around four weeks old, in your mother's womb, you grew one. A month later it had gone, dissolved as your body developed.

We all started life as a splodge like this, with a funky tail!

To see your **EYELID HOLES,** pull your bottom eyelid down very slightly and carefully, and look in a mirror. That tiny hole is a 'tear tunnel' (I just made that name up: doctors call it a lacrimal puncta). It goes from your eyes to your nose. When you cry, tears run down there. And that's why you have a runny nose when you sniffle.

The entrance to your lacrimal puncta (not actual size)

Holes (0pts) Tail 3pts

There's no point choosing something you already have!

MAKE A CRAZY CHOICE!

Discover that your pencil case is full of beetles...

OR

...find a cloud of flies in your school bag?

MAKE A CRAZY CHOICE!

Spend a week on the International Space Station with your family **OR** be the first nine year old to travel solo to the moon?

Play hide and seek with a chameleon **OR** a stick insect?

Play quidditch with Harry Potter **OR** with Draco Malfoy?

MAKE A CRAZY CHOICE!

Be a bodyguard...

OR

...a lifeguard?

MAKE A CRAZY CHOICE!

Be an eagle  a hummingbird?

Go on holiday to the pyramids of Egypt  the Great Wall of China?

Do the family laundry  do the washing up?

MAKE A CRAZY CHOICE!

Fly helicopters...

OR

...planes?

MAKE A CRAZY CHOICE!

Make people fall asleep when you click your fingers **OR** cluck like a chicken when you scratch your nose?

Have free french fries for life **OR** free chocolate?

Own a dachshund (sausage dog!) called Low Battery **OR** a gerbil called Max Power?

And you can't change their name!

MAKE A CRAZY CHOICE!

Be the most
popular
person at
the party

OR

top of
the class?

Find a
hidden well
in your
garden

OR

a tunnel
behind your
wardrobe?

Have
a year
without
rain

OR

a year
without
the sun
coming out?

MAKE A CRAZY CHOICE!

Eat earwax on crackers...

OR

...drink an earwax smoothie?

BRAINY'S TRICKY TRIVIA!

Be a storm chaser...

...a volcanologist?

see page 72

Own a pet called Frightful Flash **OR** a pet called Odor in the Court?

p75

Listen to someone screaming **OR** people clapping?

p73

Complete the biggest jigsaw puzzle you can buy **OR** the biggest Lego model?

p74

STORMS vs VOLCANOES

They're both exciting hobbies, but only one of them could **SAVE THOUSANDS OF LIVES.**

Storm chasers jump in
their car and drive towards them, hoping to predict where they're going. The goal is to witness a tornado — and survive to tell the tale.

Volcanologists explore the world's volcanoes: extinct, dormant (sleeping) and active. The big prize for these scientists would be to predict eruptions. Right now, it's just a (good) guess. Volcanoes often provide some of the best farming land available. Millions of people live near them. Knowing when to shout **RUN FOR YOUR LIVES!** would keep everybody safe.

Storms `2 pts` **Volcanoes** `6 pts`

I don't like getting wet and cold. Volcanoes win the day!

SCREAMING vs CLAPPING

If you chose someone **SCREAMING**, then what's wrong with you? It's a horrible noise. And who doesn't like the sound of someone **CLAPPING** — especially if they're applauding your *amazing dance moves?*

Give her a round of applause!

But the reason that most people will choose clapping might not be the one you think. It's the **frequency** of the noise that's the problem, not how loud it is. Our ears are much more sensitive to higher sounds (frequencies). So a scream sounds awful; but a noise with the same volume but a lower frequency, like clapping, doesn't make you want to, err, scream.

Screaming (-3 pts) **Clapping** (2 pts)

Only weirdos like the sound of screams. Clap for victory!

JIGSAW vs LEGO

Who likes jigsaws? And who likes sleeping? If your answers are YES and No, then you're in luck! Put the **world's largest jigsaw** on your birthday list. It's 60,000 pieces big, and 9m (29 feet) long — that's about as long as a bus. It's called **WHAT A WONDERFUL WORLD**. You'll need a lot of space, and even more time: more than a month without eating, drinking, or sleeping.

Feeling lazy? Try the 10,001 piece **LEGO** model of the **EIFFEL TOWER,** the biggest Lego model ever. It's about the same height as you and costs more than £500/$600. And all the pictures are in French.*

*Not really. That's just me being silly AGAIN.

Jigsaw `7 pts` **Lego** `5 pts`

A puzzle as big as a bus? You deserve the points!

FRIGHTFUL vs ODOR

If you went for Frightful Flash, you're now the proud owner of a
racing greyhound!
(She had puppies with another dog

Here's Frightful looking graceful

called *Tom's the Best!*)

ODOR IN THE COURT has a funny name, too. But you wouldn't laugh at the $30,000 this American *racehorse* won.
(You are allowed to snigger at the names of this horse's parents though: they were **FAFFY G** and **JUDGE SMELLS**.)

A horse, drawn by someone who's not very good at drawing horses

Frightful `3 pts`   Odor `4 pts`

*If you just can't choose, try my kids' bedrooms:
I can usually find a Frightful Odor in there.*

MAKE A CRAZY CHOICE!

Grow a fin like a shark...

OR

...gills like a fish?

MAKE A CRAZY CHOICE!

Go face to face with a spitting cobra  race a rhino with a 100m head start?

Live in a land where only men are allowed to make the rules  only women?

Reduce gravity  choose when the sun goes down?

MAKE A CRAZY CHOICE!

Go on holiday with your head teacher **OR** a politician?

Explore space with your family **OR** your friends?

Discover an ever-lasting battery **OR** a straw that makes drinks last forever?

Create a tornado by running in circles...

OR

...an earthquake by stamping your feet?

MAKE A CRAZY CHOICE!

Stay awake for 24 hours...

OR

...sleep for 24 hours?

MAKE A CRAZY CHOICE!

Join Rosa Parks on the bus **OR** join Nelson Mandela on his walk to freedom?

Live with 100 puppies **OR** 100 kittens?

Train as an astronomer but get a job as a chef **OR** train as a chef but get a job as an astronomer?

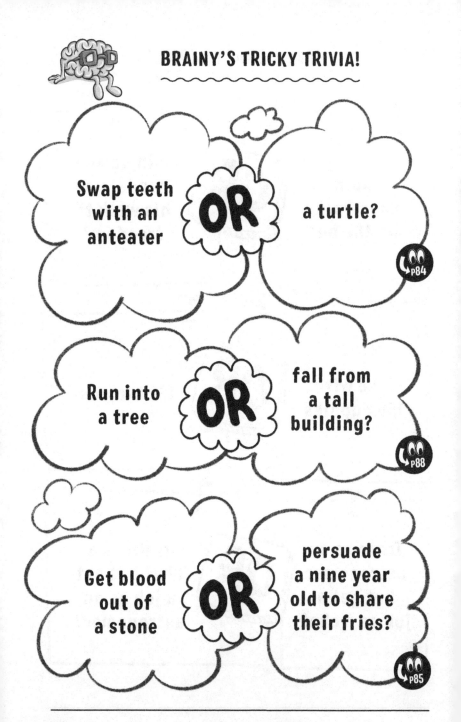

Swap teeth with an anteater **OR** a turtle?
→ p84

Run into a tree **OR** fall from a tall building?
→ p88

Get blood out of a stone **OR** persuade a nine year old to share their fries?
→ p85

BRAINY'S TRICKY TRIVIA!

Be given a baby panda...

OR

...a baby tiger?

see page 86

ANTEATER vs TURTLE

If you choose the anteater, you'll also get a sticky, **SPINY TONGUE** that's around 60cm (2ft) long. Thrust it into an ant nest. Eating 30,000 of the little critters in a day is normal! But you won't **CRUNCH** up those anty mouthfuls, because anteaters don't have any teeth.

 Instead they swallow rocks and wait for the stones to mash up their ant dinner instead!

Turtles don't have gnashers either. They rip up their food with their beaks and crush it: no teeth required. But baby turtles have a **HARD BUMP** that works like a tooth. They use it to break out of their egg, and

 then it disappears. Guess what it's called? An **EGG-TOOTH,** of course!

Anteater (0 pts) **Turtle** (1 pt)

Whichever you pick you'll save a fortune on toothpaste!

STONE vs FRIES

They're both impossible. OK, so I haven't tried squeezing a stone, but I'm sure I wouldn't get a drop of blood out of one. But I have spent a year trying to find ways to get a nine year old to share their fries. The result?

"MUMMY! DADDY'S STEALING MY CHIPS AGAIN!"

Every time. And then she turned ten. I'm still trying, though.

The 'blood out of a stone' saying is an **idiom:** words with one meaning that we now use to mean another. So I if say that something is 'like getting blood out of a stone', I mean you have no chance!

Stone (0 pts) **Fries** (0 pts)

Everyone here loses (unless you're the one with chips).

TIGER vs PANDA

Aaah, what could be **CUTER** than a baby tiger? Born blind and helpless, they need all the love, attention and milk you can give them. After about ten days their eyes will open, **SHINING BRIGHT BLUE** before slowly changing to **GOLD**. Around six weeks they'll take their first nibble of meat as they tumble and play with anyone that's around. Aaah! So cute so cuddly I wanna

oh. By three months your tiger could **SLICE YOU OPEN** with a swipe of its claws. By six months they're as big as your Dad and could kill you in a trice. Gulp.

Tell that to the man in New York who raised a pet tiger in his apartment for two years. The police used darts to tranquillize Ming (the tiger, not the owner) and take him out on a stretcher (the tiger, not the owner). Oh, and they found an alligator in there, too.

Yes, it's far better to get a panda. They're just the size of a pack of butter when they're born — how adorable! You could slip one in your pocket and take him to the movies!

Fast-forward four years. You now have a 150kg friend — the same as two regular Dads, or one big one. He poops **40 TIMES A DAY,** including in his sleep (the panda, not your Dad).

There's another panda-shaped problem, too: it's illegal to buy a panda, and every panda in the world is owned by China. So now you know (and I've saved you a fortune in bamboo pet food).

Tiger (-5 pts) Panda (-3 pts)
Have you thought about getting a dog instead?

RUN vs FALL

Running into a tree is a bad idea unless you're a woodpecker. They bang their dinky heads into trees 12,000 times a day. If you did it once, you'd get a headache. So why do you never see woodpeckers with **CRASH HELMETS?**

These little devils have a bone that wraps around their brain to stop it moving, and the shock gets spread over their body. (Still, the energy heats them up; that's why they keep stopping, to cool down.)

What about a big fall? Humans are rubbish at this, but cats are excellent. If they fall from a high building they often survive because they twist in the air and land on all four feet. And THAT is why you never see a cat with a **parachute.**

Run `3 pts` **Fall** `6 pts`

You'd look silly headbanging. Be cool: fall like a cat.

MAKE A CRAZY CHOICE!

Play pool with a breadstick and peas...

OR

...golf with a walking stick and a potato?

MAKE A CRAZY CHOICE!

Sneeze to give yourself a haircut...

CHOO!

OR

...to change into your pyjamas?

MAKE A CRAZY CHOICE!

Take a spelling test every week at school  take all the tests on your 10th birthday?

Be pictured on a postage stamp  have a statue of you in your hometown?

Make tracks in fresh snow  footprints on a beach?

MAKE A CRAZY CHOICE!

Sleep in a bath filled with the last thing you ate

OR

eat it every meal for the next month?

Find out that a neighbour came to the door with a free games console but your parent said no

OR

find out that you missed your best friend's party because you forgot?

Have a million pounds (or dollars) to spend on insects

OR

on plants?

MAKE A CRAZY CHOICE!

Run the Olympics 400m hurdles on the back of a kangaroo...

...on a giant frog?

BRAINY'S TRICKY TRIVIA!

Unlock a phone with your face...

OR

...with your tongue?

see page 96

BRAINY'S TRICKY TRIVIA!

Live for a year with no news **OR** only good news?
↪ P97

Keep a straight face **OR** a stiff upper lip?
↪ P98

Live in Damp **OR** Diaperville?
↪ P96

FACE vs TONGUE

Your face can unlock a modern phone. But it's just one of the unique ways to identify you, called your **BIOMETRICS.** Can you think of any others?

Fingerprints, of course. But also your voice, eyes and even your uniquely patterned tongue. So why don't we use that to unlock our phones? Because phones have ten times more germs on them than toilet seats. **Yurrrrrgh!**

Face **2 pts** Tongue **-3 pts**

Keep your tongue away from phones (and toilets!)

DAMP vs DIAPERVILLE

Damp is in Germany. Diaperville is in Wisconsin, USA. That's good, because nobody likes a damp diaper.

Damp **0 pts** Diaperville **1pt**

Diaperville is funny. Damp just sounds uncomfortable.

NO NEWS vs GOOD NEWS

BAD NEWS spreads much faster than **GOOD NEWS**. There's something about bad news that makes us want to know more, even though we know it might make us miserable. People say they want more good news... but then they read the bad news. Strange!

So what about **A WORLD WITHOUT ANY NEWS?** This isn't possible because things happen every day, somewhere in the world. But on a day 90 years ago, when the BBC decided that nothing important had

 happened, the news reader announced,

"There is no news."

They played piano music instead. Nobody knows or remembers if that made people happier, or more angry!

No news (-2 pts) **Good news** (3 pts)

'No news is good news,' people say. Not in this book!

FACE vs LIP

This is a **DOUBLE-IDIOM TRICK QUESTION**. (You might need a fake moustache.)

Have you ever had trouble *keeping a straight face?* A face that doesn't go wonky, stretchy or twitchy? Keeping a straight face can be pretty hard, especially when Tim Trombone, the terrible tennis teacher, **TOOTS TUNEFULLY**.

But if that teacher tells you off, your cheeks might wobble and your top lip might quiver. You can hide it behind a *bushy moustache* if you have one (do you?). Try any trick you know to stop yourself from crying!

So keeping a straight face is for happy times. Keeping a stiff upper lip is what you do when times are tough!

Face `5 pts` **Lip** `2 pts`

Laughing is better than crying (and moustaches are tickly).

MAKE A CRAZY CHOICE!

Open a banana with your toes...

...eat an apple between your elbows?

MAKE A CRAZY CHOICE!

Be a world champion toe wrestler **OR** a world champ cycleball player?

Both of these are now real sports: you score with your wheels in cycleball!

Make friends with any film star **OR** your favourite YouTuber?

Eat a chocolate cake like Bruce Bogtrotter **OR** drink George's Marvellous Medicine?

Own your own private roller coaster  a pool with a giant water slide?

Be a rhino  a vulture?

Be afraid of wheels  be afraid of fingernails?

MAKE A CRAZY CHOICE!

Eat peas with a fork...

OR

...sweetcorn with a knife?

MAKE A CRAZY CHOICE!

Take Yuri Gagarin's place as the first person in space...

OR

...take Neil Armstrong's place as the first person on the moon?

MAKE A CRAZY CHOICE!

Forget how to write **OR** forget how to run?

Learn your times tables in French **OR** run 10k?

Live in an attic **OR** a cellar?

MAKE A CRAZY CHOICE!

Be able to fly at 1000mph for an hour **OR** swim at 500mph for a day?

Have Google Maps inside your head **OR** Wikipedia?

Eat the nicest food on your plate first **OR** save it until the end?

MAKE A CRAZY CHOICE!

Collect worms to sell to anglers...

OR

...clean the monkey house at the zoo?

BRAINY'S TRICKY TRIVIA!

Try to stay dry by running for cover when it starts to rain...

OR

...walk, so you don't hit any more raindrops?

see page 110

CRAZY CHOICES FOR **9** YEAR OLDS

Live in a world without sadness **OR** without chocolate?

P112

Be afraid of knees **OR** long words?

P111

Find a skeleton in your Dad's wardrobe **OR** smell a rat?

P114

RUN vs WALK

Duh, it's obvious: run for it!

But think about it this way. If you stay still, the rain **PLOPS ON YOUR HEAD**. But if you run, you whack into raindrops from the side. So what should you do?

It's a brain-busting mixture of maths and physics, and you'll need lots of **parallelepipeds.** And if you only learn one new word in this book, make it this one. It's what a maths teacher thinks you look like when you're running fast: a leaning block made of six parallelograms. It proves two things.

(1) if you stand still, you'll never get home.

(2) if you run, you'll hit extra rain — but you'll still have drier pants. You were right all along — it's best to run!

A parallelepiped (pa-ra-lell-e-pie-ped)

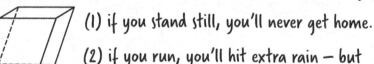

Run 7 pts **Walk** 2 pts

Walkers get soggy. Runners get hot chocolate.

KNEES vs LONG WORDS

Everyone is afraid of something. And if you're really afraid of it — you shudder and shake, even if you see a picture or think about it — then that's a PHOBIA. Pteromerhanophobia is the strange name for a common phobia: **THE FEAR OF FLYING.** But some phobias are more unusual.

Being afraid of knees sounds funny, but not if it's you that terrified by **knobbly bits!** It has a name, too: genuphobia. It's not just knees: there's a phobia for most body parts.

But if long words make you sweat, stop reading now. Because the phobia you might have is...

hippopotomonstrosesquippedaliophobia.

Even the name of the phobia is frightening!

Knees `5 pts` **Long Words** `4 pts`

Genuphobics kneed all the help they can get!

SADNESS vs CHOCOLATE

Living without chocolate would be tough. And living without sadness would be lovely, wouldn't it? But...

HOLD ON A SECOND!

If you live in China, you probably live very well without chocolate already. The average Chinese person eats around **70g** of chocolate each year: that's just one **SMALL CHOCOLATE BAR**. Imagine if you could only eat one Milky Way or Mars bar each year!

Now hop over to Tahiti, a beautiful island in the Pacific where a girl's grandad has just died. Can you imagine how **sad** she feels? You probably can... but she doesn't feel sad. She might feel **STRANGE**, or **SICK**, but not "sad" – because Tahitians don't have that word in their language.

But do you need a word to feel something? Which of these theories do you agree with?

1) You can only **FEEL** something if you have a word for it. So you might be **MISERABLE,** or **UPSET,** but you can't be sad if you've never heard the word.

2) The feeling always exists, with or without a word. You just don't know what to call it!

Famous authors **DOUGLAS ADAMS** and **JOHN LLOYD** wrote a book all about (2). They invented names for feelings that everyone knows, but doesn't talk about. But what to call them? They chose the names of English villages! So that odd feeling when you sit on a chair or a toilet, and the seat is warm from the previous person? That's called **SHOEBURYNESS!**

Sadness 8pts **Chocolate** 3pts

Whatever the word, let's make the world a happy place!

SKELETON vs RAT

It's double-idiom time again!

Most people think that rats are pretty unlovable, and they certainly don't want to sniff one because they can really **pong.** (So would you if you ate out of the bins). So if you smell a rat, you've got a whiff of something unpleasant.

What is it? Could it be something fishy in your Dad's wardrobe? ('Something fishy' is an idiom which means something suspicious.) He might have secrets in there — like a skeleton!

So if someone has a skeleton in the cupboard or closet, they have an old secret they don't want you to

know. And sometimes it's better that way, so don't go snooping around!

Skeleton (-2pts) **Rat** (2pts)

Leave those skeletons to rest in peace!

MAKE A CRAZY CHOICE!

Get sunburn...

OR

...have a headache?

MAKE A CRAZY CHOICE!

Spend all day at the hairdressers  **in a supermarket?**

Wake up with different colour hair every morning  **hair that washes itself?**

Drive a car made of seaweed  **cheese?**

MAKE A CRAZY CHOICE!

Wear chocolate underpants...

OR

...jelly socks?

MAKE A CRAZY CHOICE!

Have a wrinkly face...

OR

...a wrinkly bottom?

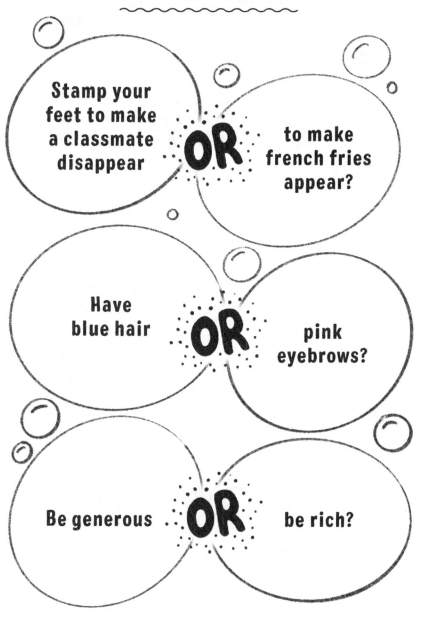

Stamp your feet to make a classmate disappear **OR** to make french fries appear?

Have blue hair **OR** pink eyebrows?

Be generous **OR** be rich?

MAKE A CRAZY CHOICE!

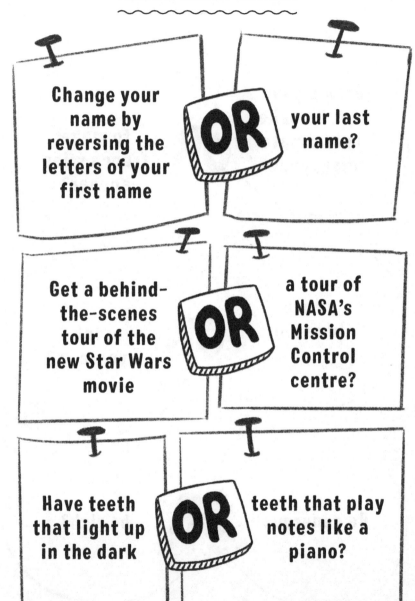

Change your name by reversing the letters of your first name **OR** your last name?

Get a behind-the-scenes tour of the new Star Wars movie **OR** a tour of NASA's Mission Control centre?

Have teeth that light up in the dark **OR** teeth that play notes like a piano?

Grow claws like an eagle...

OR

...webbed feet like a duck?

MAKE A CRAZY CHOICE!

Send one of your teachers into space

OR

make a school subject illegal?

Attack

OR

defend?

Be able to give your Dad a piggyback

OR

gleek whenever you want?

Someone who can gleek can shoot a jet of saliva out of their mouth. It sometimes happens when you yawn!

BRAINY'S TRICKY TRIVIA!

Take another school trip – this time to a Mustard Museum  the Shoe Lace Museum?

 p132

Walk like an Egyptian  walk on stilts like a palm tree?

 p128

Live without your appendix  your nose hair?

 p126

Play Happy Birthday on a nose flute...

OR

...an ear trumpet?

see page 130

APPENDIX vs NOSE HAIR

If you thought an *appendix* was an extra bit at the end, that you probably don't need, you're right. And that works if you're thinking of the appendix of *a book,* or **YOUR** appendix. This is a little tube in your body, about the size

> If I took your appendix out, this is what your scar would look like.

of a finger. It's attached to your large intestine on the right of your tummy. What is it for? Who knows. It might store good bacteria, but one thing is for certain: if it gets badly infected, the doctors will take it out and you'll never have to think about it again.

You probably don't think much about nose hair, but it's something you're going to get, whether you like it or not! It's a little forest of fine hairs, all coated in mucus (SNOT), waiting to trap any dirt or beasties that

CRAWL UP YOUR HOOTER. Sure, you could live without it, but then all that dirt would end up in your lungs. Not good.

As you get older, those nose hairs keep growing, and keep getting thicker. Long ones tend to fall out, but sometimes you'll see a tuft of them sticking out of your grandpa's nose.

If you want to see a grown man cry, wait until he nods off in his armchair and give those nose hairs

a gentle tweak. But don't blame me if he is also unspeakably cross and **never speaks to you again.**

Appendix 2pts **Nose Hair** (-1pt)

Old men just wouldn't be the same without nose hair!

EGYPTIAN vs TREE

Back in the dark ages, when your parents were born, there was a song in the charts

TRICK QUESTION

called **WALK LIKE AN EGYPTIAN** by a group called The Bangles. In the video, people did this crazy sideways walk with their hands sticking out at *funny angles,* just like the people in ancient Egyptian paintings.

Here's someone not walking like an Egyptian

Except... that's just the way the artists painted them! Egyptians walked normally, as far as we can tell.

So who **DOES** 'walk like an Egyptian'? According to the man who wrote the song, it's people on ferries on a rough sea crossing, trying to get down the corridors as the ship lurches from side to side. This sounds 100% ridiculous to me, but then I've never tried it.

What about palm trees? Surely they don't walk on stilts? In **DEEPEST, DARKEST ECUADOR,** a special palm tree grows on special roots, just like stilts. And one botanist reported that they could move several centimetres each year, towards better soil, using these stilts. Cool! Everyone got very excited, and filled the internet with articles about it. Except... other scientists came along and said that was a load of old cobblers.

NOTE TO MAT FROM THE EDITOR: Egyptians that walk NORMALLY? Trees that DON'T walk? The sun rises, all 9 year olds pick their noses... tell me something new!

Here's a palm tree that doesn't walk

Egyptian (0pts) **Tree** (0pts)

Let's pretend this page never happened. I'm so sorry.

FLUTE vs TRUMPET

If you chose to entertain your family with a **nose flute,** congratulations! In parts of Africa and the Pacific Islands you could probably form a band, as nose flutes are pretty popular there. Hold the instrument to a nostril, plug the other nostril closed and you're ready to rock!

But if you picked an **ear trumpet,** you've been tricked! Ear trumpets were used for hundreds of years by people who couldn't hear well. (The composer Ludwig van Beethoven even had one!)

SCIENCE ALERT: when you speak to a friend with cups and string, you make the air in the cup **VIBRATE** with your voice. The vibrations travel along the string and into the air in the other cup. And when **THAT** air vibrates, they can hear you!

Keep the string tight so that the vibrations travel better!

An ear trumpet directs sound, too. The user holds the narrow end to their ear, with the flared end pointing towards the person who is talking. Sound waves bounce down the tube and suddenly, *granny can hear again!* You don't see ear trumpets any more because scientists worked out how to put the whole contraption inside the ear — we call them **HEARING AIDS.**

Sound travels as a wave of vibrating particles. In air, these waves bounce off surfaces so you can direct the sound

So what would happen if you tried to play an ear trumpet? You'd most likely get a mouthful of your great grandad's earwax! *URGH!*

Flute 3 pts **Trumpet** -2 pts
Maybe you could start a nose flute band in school!

MUSTARD vs LACES

If the Museum of Underwear on page 30 didn't float your boat, then perhaps you should head to the *Mustard Museum* in Wisconsin, USA? I've heard it's hot stuff!

Even better: it actually exists, unlike the Shoe Lace Museum, which I just made up.

Hang on a second, the phone is ringing.

"WHAT'S THAT? REALLY? SURE, I'LL TELL THEM."

I'm back with good news. Visit the City Museum in St Louis, USA, and there's a shoelace factory where you can see laces being made in a zillion different colours! It sounds brilliant, but is mustard better than shoelaces? Let's call it a tie!*

Mustard **3 pts** Laces **3 pts**

Worst joke ever. Best place to end this book!

BRAINY'S SCORECARD

Player ❶ .... **Player ❷** ....

Page		SCORE ❶	❷	Page		SCORE ❶	❷
10	Cockroach vs Forehead			74	Jigsaw vs Lego		
11	Runway vs Zoo			75	Frightful vs Odor		
12	Trees vs Stars			84	Anteater vs Turtle		
13	General vs Major			85	Stone vs Fries		
26	Dolphin vs Snail			86	Tiger vs Panda		
27	Wolf vs Angel			88	Run vs Fall		
28	Rhubarb vs Sub			96	Face vs Tongue		
30	Socks vs Underpants			96	Damp vs Diaperville		
40	Donkey vs Rat			97	No News vs Good News		
41	Speed Up vs Slo-Mo			98	Face vs Lip		
42	Brown vs Green			110	Run vs Walk		
43	Kitchen vs Bathroom			111	Knees vs Long Words		
54	War vs Basketball			112	Sadness vs Chocolate		
56	Skyscraper vs Parrot			114	Skeleton vs Rat		
58	Wolf vs Sumo			126	Appendix vs Nose Hair		
60	Holes vs Tail			128	Egyptian vs Tree		
72	Storms vs Volcanoes			130	Flute vs Trumpet		
73	Screaming vs Clapping			132	Mustard vs Laces		
	TOTAL:				GRAND TOTAL:		

One Last Crazy Choice!

I hoped you enjoyed making all these crazy choices. And now you also know more about panda cubs, giant jigsaws, volcanoes and sumo wrestlers. One day, you'll thank me for that.*

Here's your last head scratcher: will you keep this book a secret? Or will you find a way to give your opinion to everyone you know, and millions more you don't? Grown-ups do this all the time – why shouldn't you?

If you have something to say, ask a parent to leave a review wherever they bought this book. (You may need to write it for them – you know what grown-ups are like.)

I can't wait to find out what you think!

*When you're waiting for your first Sumo match, doing a jigsaw with your pet panda by your side, and you hear the rumble of a volcano about to erupt. It'll happen one day, believe me.

Three More to Try!

Awesome Jokes That Every 9 Year Old Should Know
The best-selling series of jokes that grown-ups love to hear first thing in the morning.

The Cheeky Charlie series
Meet Harriet and her small, stinky brother. Together, they're trouble. Fabulously funny capers for chaos-loving kids!

Fantastic Wordsearches for 9 Year Olds
Wordsearch puzzles with a difference: themed, crossword clues and hidden words await!

Order online or in bookshops, or discover more at
www.matwaugh.co.uk

My Life of Choices

I've made some terrible choices in my life.

✈ When I was six, I dribbled modelling glue on the radiator. I planned to peel it off later (very satisfying). But I forgot, and sat in it instead.

🏠 When I was nine, I dropped an epic water balloon from a bedroom window at my friend's house. It fell inside the house, not outside. It was his parents' bedroom.

🏊 When I was sixteen, I skipped breakfast. In assembly I fainted and fell head-first into a row of children three years below me. I can still hear them laughing.

But then I grew up and I started making excellent decisions!

🐘 I decided that an African elephant wasn't flapping its ears to be friendly, and that we should run. Fast.

🎢 I took a trip to a theme park where I met Mrs Waugh. She wasn't called that then, of course. That would be weird.

✚ I did home improvements in flip-flops. Actually, forget that one: I had to visit hospital with a rusty nail sticking out of my foot. The nurses said that it served me right, and that men of my age shouldn't wear flip-flops.

See? I'm super-wise now, and my family agree (they don't).

What's the best and worst decision *you've* ever made? I'd love to hear from you – your parents can email me!

mail@matwaugh.co.uk

Made in the USA
Las Vegas, NV
10 April 2024

88516977R00080